Foreword

This book aims to help proficient descant recorder players who are capable readers to transfer to treble. It teaches no rudiments and little, directly, in the way of technique, assuming that such information has already been acquired while learning descant. It is therefore totally unsuitable for beginners who wish to play treble first, and they are referred to the other treble tutors in this series* in which all the necessary technical and reading skills are systematically and progressively developed.

The treble, the true solo recorder, is a rich and satisfying instrument with an extensive repertoire of fine music. A knowledge of its fingering, coupled with your present ability on descant, will open the way to playing all other C and F recorders, immediately increasing, out of all proportion to the effort involved, your opportunities for music-making and the pleasure you will derive from it.

Whether you play as soloist, as member of a consort or in a larger ensemble I am certain you will gain great satisfaction from your treble and I wish you many, many hours of pleasure.

Brian Bonsor

*'Enjoy the Recorder', Treble Tutor Books 1 and 2 (ED 11468 and ED 11470).

Using this Book

If you have tried even a few notes on your new treble you will have discovered some of the more obvious differences from your descant — the greater size and weight, the wider spacing of the finger holes and the need for slightly more breath to fill the instrument.

But you may also have made a much more important discovery — that the sequence of fingerings learned on your descant works equally well on treble and that any tune you know on descant can, with the same fingerings, be played on treble *though it will sound lower.* This pitch difference is the only real stumbling-block to moving smoothly from descant to treble for, unfortunately, it means that notes you already know very well on descant must now be fingered quite differently on treble:

These new fingerings are best learned by treating the treble as a completely new instrument and, from the very beginning, playing from notation **without ever thinking of, or referring to, your descant.** (Some teachers go further and make their pupils abandon their descants completely for several weeks, but I have seldom found this necessary.) You will be pleasantly surprised to find that the muscular memory developed in your descant playing will still guide your fingers in the right direction in treble tunes which move mainly by step (i.e. to the nearest note above or below). Difficulties usually arise only when sizeable leaps suddenly appear or — and this is less commonly realised — when the music, by its position on the stave, has a strong 'look' of descant music, the brain tending at such moments to recall the fingering it knows best.

It is therefore vital to be able *instantly* to link a note with its new fingering and, as this can only be achieved by **regular and repeated practice** of the commonest leaps, I have devised two useful, if somewhat unmusical, aids for this purpose — the **Practice Circle** (page 22) and the **Recognition Square** (page 20).

As each new note is introduced it is placed in the centre of a Practice Circle and surrounded by the notes most frequently associated with it. Moving at random from notes in the outer circle to the new note and back gives considerable practice in the commoner intervals involving that note.

ENJOY THE RECORDER
A comprehensive method for group, individual and self-tuition

In gratitude, to my friend
Herbert Hersom
who sowed the seed

FROM DESCANT TO TREBLE

- by -

BRIAN BONSOR

PART 1

ED 12229

Mainz · London · Berlin · Madrid · New York · Paris · Prague · Tokyo · Toronto

© 1987 Schott Music Ltd, London
ED 12229 · S&Co. 8750
ISMN 979-0-2201-1422-9
ISBN 978-0-946535-01-9

Text setting by: Furlonger Phototext Ltd, Bournemouth
Illustrations by: Derrick Smith
Design by: Geoffrey Wadsley

Recognition Squares, on the other hand, provide a constantly changing succession of *totally unrelated* notes and, especially at speed, demand secure and instant recognition for success. **N.B. Students working without a teacher are advised to stop frequently on a note and make certain that the fingering is correct,** for it is vital to avoid practising mistakes.

As a further aid, tunes are systematically grouped to give concentrated practice on the specific interval shown in the **heading** to each group:

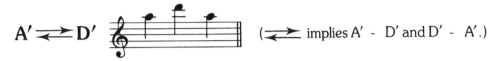

Before attempting any tune, look back to the appropriate heading and play the interval *from the notation* two or three times to fix both the look of the note and its fingering in your mind. Note that throughout this book fingers are identified as follows:

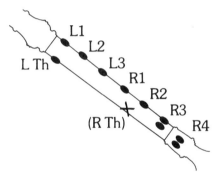

The regular practice of **scales and arpeggios** is essential for building a sound technique. Practise them in several different ways — with every note tongued, slurred overall and with a variety of different tonguings and rhythms:

Technical exercises (e.g. 138, 139, 143) should be practised tongued and slurred unless otherwise indicated.

The extra weight of the treble (particularly a wooden treble) makes some form of additional support almost essential, either a thumb-rest (which any instrument repairer will fit — though corks and rubber bands have been pressed into service!) or the use of R4 on the end-joint beading between holes R3 and R4. (See illustration) If this use of R4 as a supporting finger is new to you, seize every opportunity to try it out in the early pages of the book and you will soon acquire an extremely valuable habit which will show its real worth later in fast passages using mainly the fingers of the left hand and jumping quickly from octave to octave.

Such passages abound in a number of particularly testing tunes included as a challenge at the end of several sections. The brave may decide to tackle them immediately, but they can equally well be reserved for later practice. Schools may choose to ignore them completely for, even without them, there is ample material at each stage to give young players a thorough grounding in the moves they are most likely to need.

A final word. Do not try to move on too quickly — and certainly not before any hesitancy over a new note has disappeared. Time spent on the earlier stages will be richly rewarded. Press on too quickly and you will soon find you have built on sand.

Now, pick up your treble — and let's make a start!

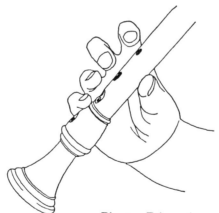

Placing R4 on the end-joint beading between holes R3 and R4 will help to keep the recorder steady, but be careful that R4 does not accidentally shade one or both of its holes or some notes will be slightly out of tune.

If I tell you that  **produces the note C** , **try, without any further**

information, to play the following tune:

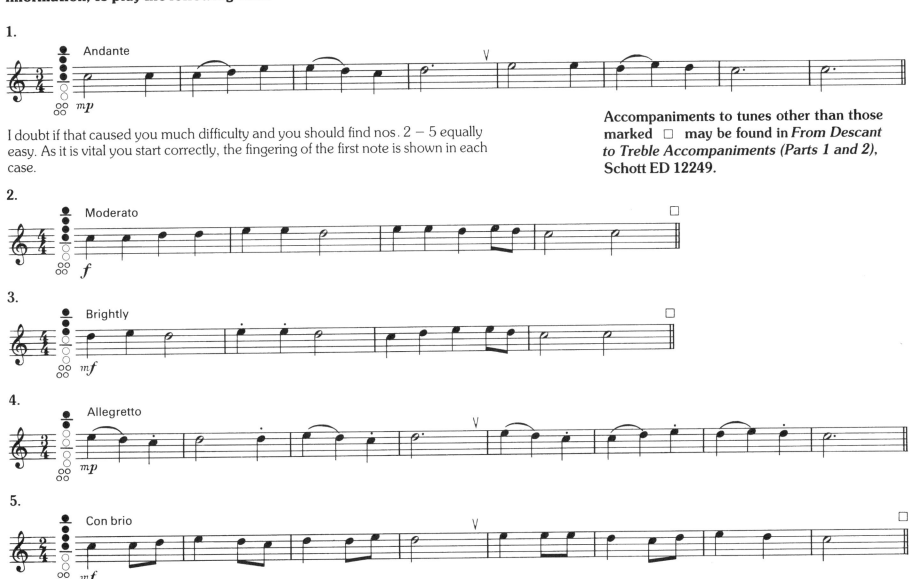

I doubt if that caused you much difficulty and you should find nos. 2 – 5 equally easy. As it is vital you start correctly, the fingering of the first note is shown in each case.

Accompaniments to tunes other than those marked □ may be found in *From Descant to Treble Accompaniments (Parts 1 and 2)*, Schott ED 12249.

From tunes 1 – 5 you have learned the fingerings for C, D and E:

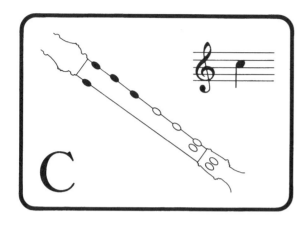

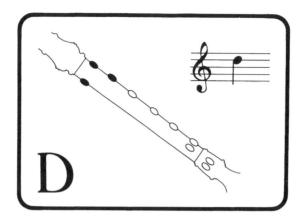

These tunes always moved by step (i.e. to the nearest note up or down). Tunes 6 – 9
introduce the first tiny leap:

Before tackling each of the following tunes come back
to this heading and, **from the notation,** play
E – C – E several times. **Use all headings
throughout the book in this way.** (See page 5)

6.

Briskly

7. Who's dat yonder?

Allegro

☐ **Negro Spiritual**

8.

Andantino

(V)

9.

Play slowly up the three notes you have just learned:

Here they are again, but this time let your fingers take you on to the next two notes:

   How did you finger: [and] ?

Yes!   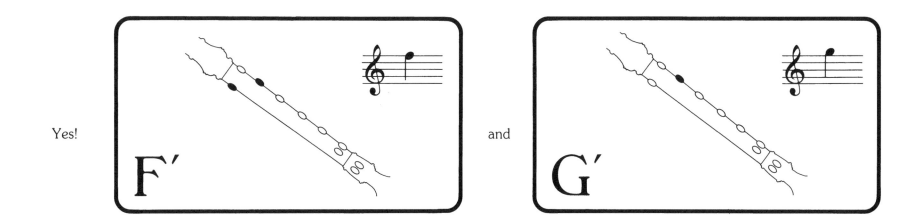   and

Now try the following tunes, **but take time in every case to check the fingering of the first note.**

10. Les Bouffons (part) (used also in the middle section of no. 20)

11.

12. The little apprentice shepherd-boy

13. Winter song

14. German folk-song

15. Patsy-Atsy-Ory-Ay

16. **Le Roi Dagobert**

French

17. **Sonatina in C major (part)**

Diabelli/Bergmann

*Omit grace-notes ad lib.

Although there is more fine solo music for the treble than for any other recorder, it also has an important role as a lower or inner part in a recorder ensemble. Playing in parts is a particularly satisfying way to make music and to give you some experience of it and to enable you to enjoy playing with a friend this book contains several two-part settings, a few in this section for descant and treble, the rest for two trebles. Note that in nos. 18 – 20 the treble plays the *lower* line.

Playing in Parts

18. **Gavotte III (part) (from 'Easy Lessons')**

☐ Hook/Bergmann

19. Now the day is over (Eudoxia)

S. Baring-Gould

20. Les Bouffons (part)

French

ritard. (last time only)   Fine

D.C. al Fine

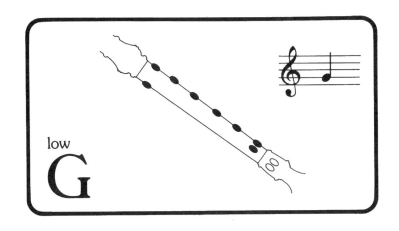

G

Three new leaps:

(a) G ⇄ C   (b) G ⇄ D   (c) G ⇄ G′

21. This exercise includes all these leaps. Practise it thoroughly.

Firmly

f

22. The Bogeyman

Con brio

1.   2.

German

mf

23. C'est un petit oiseau

Not too fast

□ French

mp leggiero

24. My goose

Allegro

□ English

25. A bird wished to marry

Allegretto

German

mp leggiero

26. Alouette

French-Canadian

Con brio

mf

2nd time ( ) Fine

D.C. al Fine

f

| low A | Try No. 27 and you may be surprised to find that your fingers already know how to move from low G to low A! |

27. There's a hole in the bucket

With a swing

☐ German

(V)

mf

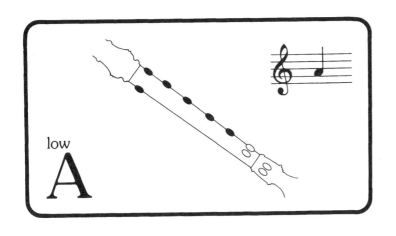

G ⇄ A

C ⇄ A

28. Nobody knows the trouble I've seen

Slowly

☐ Negro Spiritual

29. I want to sing

Con spirito

☐ Negro Spiritual

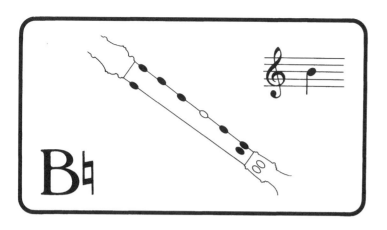

— uses the R.H. middle fingers.

(a) C ⟷ B 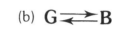   (b) G ⟷ B    (c) D ⟷ B

30. **The Arpeggio of G major**   (See page 5 for instructions on practising arpeggios)
When practising arpeggios slurred, the slur extends over the repeated bar as shown by the dotted slur.

(a)    (b)

* × 3: play the bracketed bar(s) *three* times.

31. **The Dominant 7th of C major**

(a)    (b)

Try to memorise nos. 30 and 31.

32. **Dance hither**

33. I'se the B'y

Presto

☐ Newfoundland

34. Bobby Shaftoe

Allegro vivace

☐ English

35. Oliver Cromwell   Play all on one breath!

Fast

☐ English

36. Mohrentanz (Morisco)

Boldly

Susato

Fine

2nd time

D.C. al Fine

B♮ – A – G

37.

(a)   R2 stays down

(b)   R2 down   R2 down

38. Robin Adair

Andante

Irish

39. Abend wird es wieder

Moderato

☐ J. C. H. Rinck

40. The cradle

Gently

Austrian

41. Sellenger's Round (part)

Con brio

☐ English

42. Madam, I will buy you

Giocoso

☐ Northumbrian

43. **Mein Verlangen** (part)

Moderato

Susato

mp espressivo

44. **Czech Carol**

Brightly

f

45. **The Fox**

Andantino

E. Anschütz

mp

p

mp

46. **The little wood-bird**

Allegretto

□ German

Tr. 1

mp
(Melody)

Tr. 2

mp

47. **High road to Linton**

□ Scots

RECOGNITION SQUARE – 1

– to help you recognise notes quickly. (See pages 4 and 5)

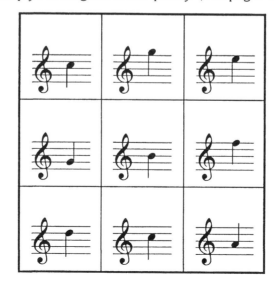

Start in any square and move, continuously and at random, to the nearest square in any direction –up, down, forwards, backwards, or diagonally. Stop from time to time to check that your fingering is correct.

Begin slowly and gradually increase speed.

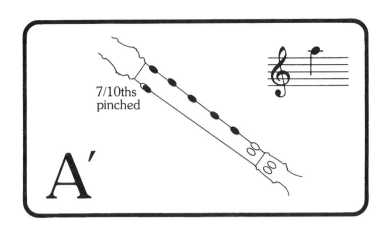

— easily recognised: on the first leger line above the staff.

— easily fingered: like low A but pinched.

A ⇌ A'      A' ⇌ G'

48.

Boldly — not too fast

49.

Moderato

* If G' − A' sounds untidy, check that all incoming fingers arrive together. Pay special attention to L3 which is often lazy.

Nos. 50 − 59 give practice in moving from G' − A'.

50.

Con brio

21

51.

PRACTICE CIRCLE
(See page 4)

— to give you concentrated practice on the commonest moves to and from A′.

From any note in the outer ring move to the central note and out again to a number of different notes at random, **returning to the central note after each.** (See diagram)

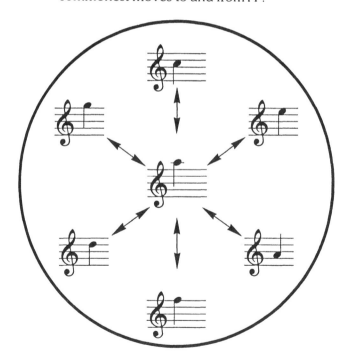

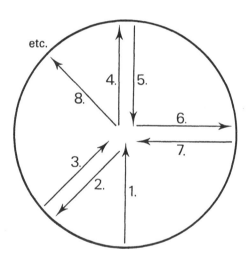

Start slowly and gradually build up speed. **Use the circle for a few minutes in every practice session.**

52. **The Saucy Sailor**

Andante

English

53. **Old Highland Air**

Gently

Scots

54. **Go tell it on the mountain**

Joyfully

☐ Negro Spiritual

2nd time (𝅗𝅥.) 𝄾) Fine

D.C. al Fine

55. Susie, little Susie

56. Wae's me for Prince Charlie

57. Guter Mond

58. Ronde (1)

59. Rigaudon

Fischer

60.

Moderato

61. Bonny at morn

Gently

Northumbrian

62. Branle

Fast

Susato

63. The Arpeggio of A minor Remember to play the music under the bracket *three* times.

64. Bohemian Carol

65.

66. Russian folk-song

67.

68. 'Christmas Pastoral' (part)

Robin Milford

69.

70. My sweetheart

German

71. Il pleut, il pleut, bergère

French

Allegretto

72. Menuet from 'Première Suite'

Bâton

tr*

V

V

V

tr

* F' – E trill

-tr

RECOGNITION SQUARE – 2

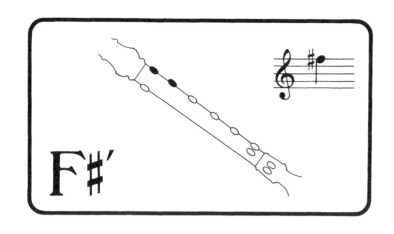

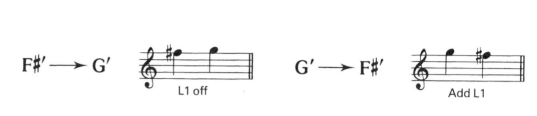

F#' → G' L1 off

G' → F#' Add L1

73. The Scale of G major (See page 5 for instructions on practising scales)

74. Chorale: Vom Himmel hoch

Maestoso   M. Luther

75. Kolyada

Gaily   □ Russian

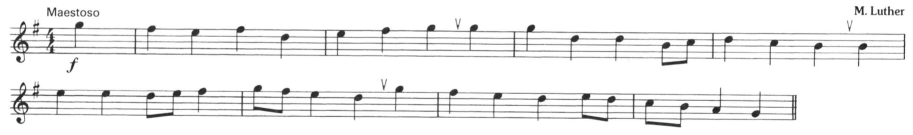

76. Barbara Allen

Gently

☐ English

77. Leaving Lishmore

With a swing

Scots

78. Stumpie (Buttered Peas)

Con spirito

☐ Scots

79. Kenmure's on and awa' (Hexham Races)

PRACTICE CIRCLE for F#′

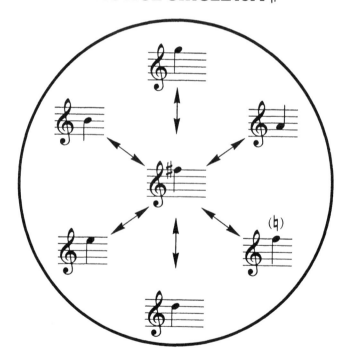

This melody uses all the moves in the practice circle:

80.

TUNES WITH F♯ AND F♮

81. Piano Trio No. 8 in G major K564 (part)

Mozart

82. Chorale: Nun danket alle Gott

☐ German

83. She is far from the land

☐ Irish

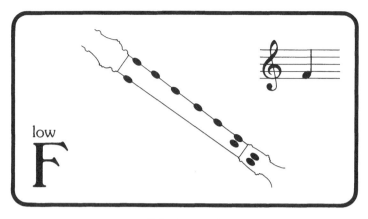

F

– all fingers on!

Although low F is easily fingered (all fingers on) and recognised (in the bottom space) it may prove awkward for some players with small hands or short fourth fingers. Begin by trying the first bar of no. 84 a few times, gradually adjusting the position of the end-joint until you feel your right little finger falling squarely and comfortably on *both* double holes. Every hole must be completely sealed if low F is to speak and breath pressure must, of course, be low. If the note fails or squeaks, suspect R3 which may have been pulled slightly out of position. Breath pressure may be at fault but this is less likely with a player of your experience.

Now try the first two exercises, which approach low F mainly by step:

G ⟶ F

84.

85.

A ⟶ F

No. 86 jumps from A to F to encourage the correct spacing of R3 and R4 *before* they reach the instrument.

86.

Here all the right-hand fingers must space themselves accurately *before* reaching the instrument.

87.

88. The Arpeggio of F major

89. Poor old maid

90. My home

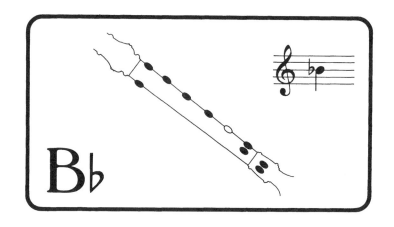

B♭

— another problem note for players with small hands or short fourth fingers.

Remember — B **f**lat is **f**orked.

B♭ is best approached at first from low F. **Raise only R2. Check that R3 and R4 remain solidly on their double holes.**

91.

repeat several times.

92.

Lively

93. Some awkward shifts. **Return to them frequently.**

Watch L3!

Play each tongued and slurred. You will find some much more difficult slurred!

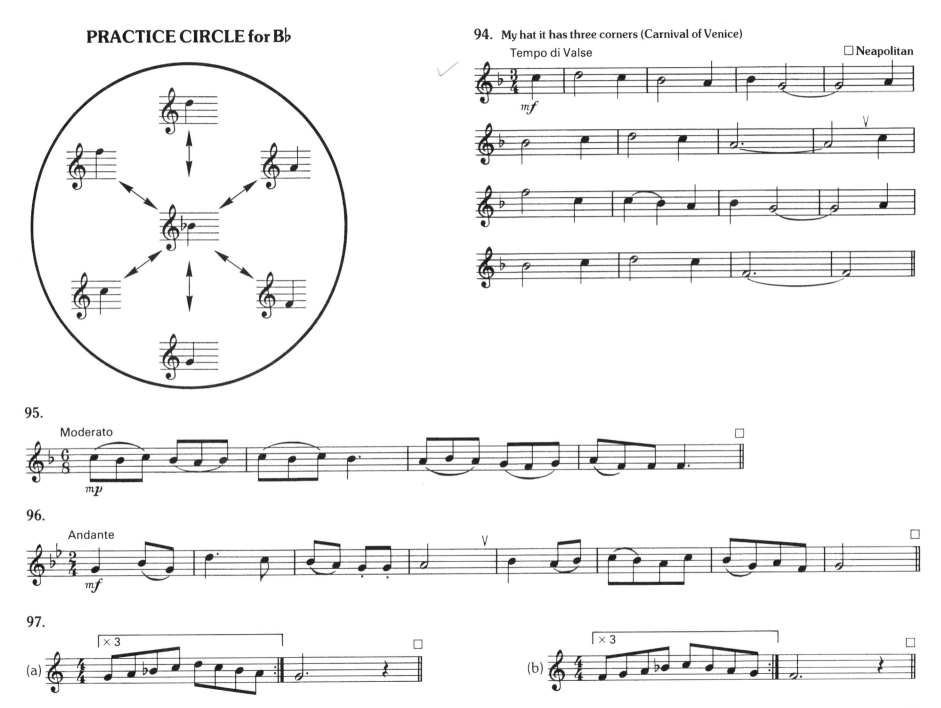

PRACTICE CIRCLE for B♭

94. My hat it has three corners (Carnival of Venice)

Tempo di Valse ☐ Neapolitan

95. Moderato

96. Andante

97.
(a) × 3
(b) × 3

98. Im Schnützelputz-Häusel

With a swing

German

99. The Scale of F major

Remember to practise all scales and arpeggios with different tonguings and in different rhythms.
(See page 5)

100. The rising of the lark

Con brio

Welsh

101. **Where lie the ox and ass**

□ French

102. **'Twas pretty to be in Balinderry**

□ Irish

103. **Small coals and little money**

□ Northumbrian

(ti - ki - ti)

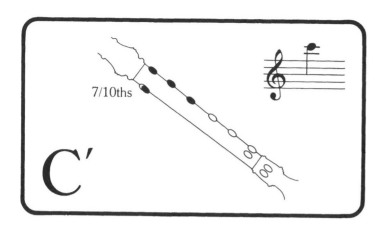

C′

7/10ths

– an easy note. Finger as for low C *and pinch* (about 7/10ths closed).

104.

105.

Con brio

f

106. The Arpeggio of C major

(a) ×3

(b) ×3

107.

Not fast – yet!

mf

PRACTICE CIRCLE for C′

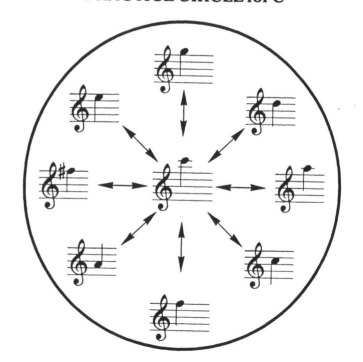

108. De lustighe Boer

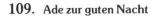

109. Ade zur guten Nacht

110. **Mein Christian**

Moderato

German

Slight stress only.

111. **German Air**

Not too fast — see bars 11 and 15!

☐ **Müller**

112. All the birds

□ German

Brightly

Tr. 1

Tr. 2

$E \longrightarrow C'$

113. I wear a little golden ring

□ German

Allegretto

mp leggiero

43

$F' \longrightarrow C'$

114. Hans im Schnakeloch

THREE TUNES FOR FUN:

115. Athole Highlanders

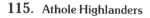

116. Davy-Davy Knick-knack

117. **Hamilton House**

Con brio

□ Scots

RECOGNITION SQUARE – 3

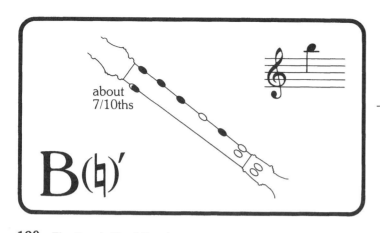

118.

− 1. Finger low B.
  2. **Remove R3** and pinch.

repeat several times.

119.

120. The Boar's Head Carol

Con spirito

f

English

121. The Scale of C major

A′ − B′ − C′

(a)

(b)

122. The Wishing Well

Allegretto

mf

French

123. Ein' feste Burg

M. Luther

124. O du fröhliche

□German

125. Ca' the ewes

Slowly

Scots

126. Rosestock, Holderblüh

Joyfully

German

127. Air from Third Suite

Bingham ed. Tilmouth

128. Sonata for Treble and Piano (part)

Semplice*

Walter Bergmann

*($\downarrow$ = c.84)

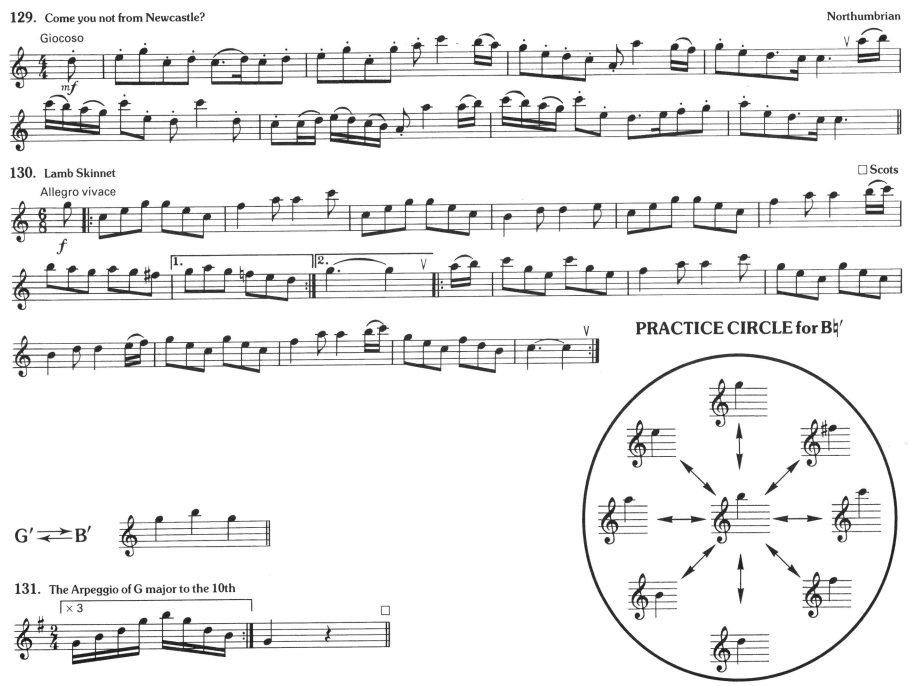

129. Come you not from Newcastle?

Northumbrian

Giocoso

130. Lamb Skinnet

☐ Scots

Allegro vivace

G′ ⇌ B′

131. The Arpeggio of G major to the 10th

× 3

PRACTICE CIRCLE for B♮′

132. Austrian Carol

133. Torry Burn

$F\sharp' \rightleftarrows B'$

134. The Arpeggio of B minor

135. The Mason's Apron

☐ Scots

RECOGNITION SQUARE – 4

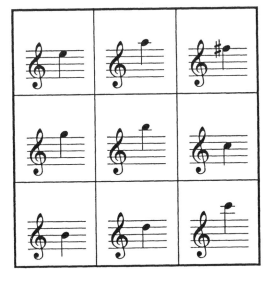

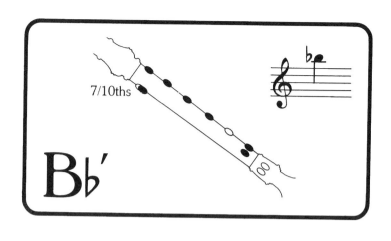

Bb'

7/10ths

— 1. Finger low Bb.
2. **Remove R4** and pinch (about 7/10ths).

136.

Repeat each exercise several times:

A' ⇌ Bb'

137.

C' ⇌ Bb'

138.

139.

Play all exercises of this type (a) tongued; (b) with a slur over the repeated bar; and (c) with varied tonguings. (See page 5)

140. Ronde: 'Wo bistu'

52

141. Strawberry Fair

Gaily

PRACTICE CIRCLE for B♭'

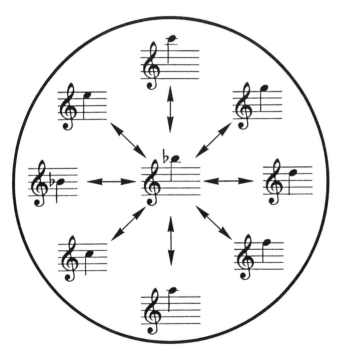

G' ⇄ B♭'

142.

143.

144. The Arpeggio of G minor to the 10th

145. O Maiden

Andante

German

146. Now is the month of Maying

Brightly

Thomas Morley

147. Mein Mädel

Very lively

□ German

148. The Soldiers have no money

Allegro – ma non troppo

□ Dutch

55

149. Cousin Michael

150. The Dominant 7th of F major

151. Down in the Lowlands

152. The Arpeggio of B♭

(a)

(b)

153. Bunessan

Gaelic

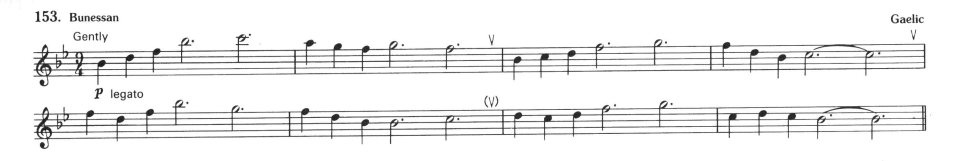

Gently

𝑝 legato

154. With care I tend my rosebush

☐ French

Allegretto

mf

D ⟶ B♭'

155. The Merry Musician

Giocoso   German

C ⟶ B♭'

156. Minuet (from Concerto Grosso Op. 6 No. 11)

Corelli

⊛ **A' – G' trill**   *originally E

157. Sarie Marais

59

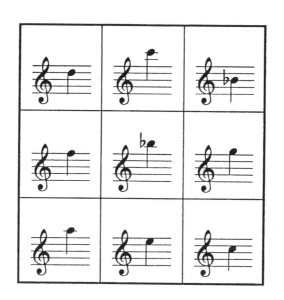

RECOGNITION SQUARE – 5

$A\sharp' = B\flat'$ — and is fingered the same way.

158.

(a)　　　　　　　　　　　　　(b)

159. Down among the dead men (part)

A♯ is briefly mentioned at this point as you will occasionally find it in otherwise simple ensemble music. More practice is given in **Part 2**.

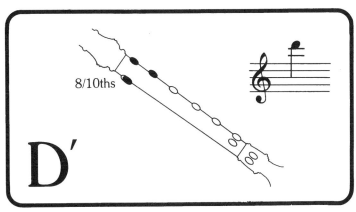

8/10ths

D′

— 1. Finger low D and pinch — about 8/10ths.
  2. Tongue precisely but not too strongly. Slightly more breath pressure may help the note to strike cleanly.

If D′ sounds a little flat (and on many instruments it will), open the thumbhole a fraction more and the pitch will rise.

D ⇌ D′

G′ ⇌ D′

160. Ma commère quand je danse

French

Allegro
mf
f   *mf*   *f*   *mf*

C′ ⇌ D′

161.

☐

162. In the fields in frosts and snows (part)

☐ English

Moderato
mp

61

163.

164. Lovely Joan

Moderato

English

165. Ein Mädchen oder Weibchen (from 'The Magic Flute') (part)

Andante

Mozart

166. How happy could I be with either (from 'The Beggar's Opera')

Allegro vivace

☐ English

Tr. 1

Tr. 2

167. Botany Bay

With a swing

☐ Australian

168. **The Times**   Old Dance Tune

Allegro

169. **Corn Rigs**   Scots

Allegretto

170. **The Blackthorn Stick**   □ Irish

Allegro vivace

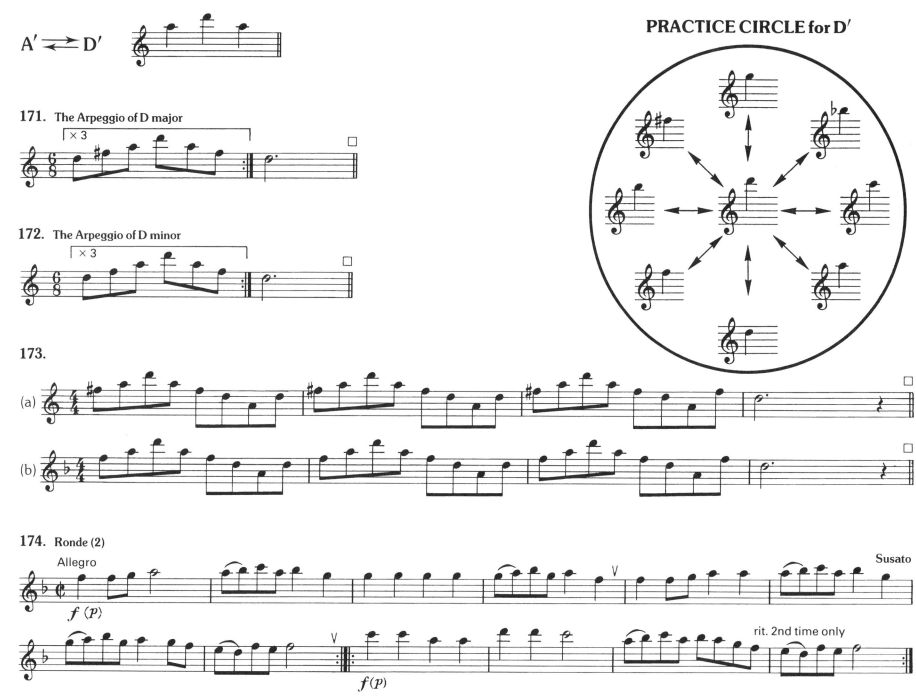

175. If all the world were paper

Giocoso

□ English

176. Over the mountains

English

Andantino

cresc.

f

177. The Queen's Dream

178. Agincourt Song

Boldly

□ English

B′ ⇌ D′

179.

180. The Arpeggio of G major to the 12th

181. The Dominant 7th of C major to the 12th

182. The Arpeggio of B minor to the 10th

183.

184. **I'd like to climb a little tree**

185. **Let us take the road (from 'The Beggar's Opera': based on March from Handel's 'Rinaldo')**

186. **Wassail**

English

68

187.

188. The Arpeggio of G minor to the 12th

189.

190. The Arpeggio of B♭ major to the 10th

191. There stands a little man

Vivace

p leggiero

2nd time

German

192. Un Cerf dans sa grande Maison

Allegretto

mf

f

French

69

193. King Arthur's servants

☐ English

194. Love brings great joy

German

$F\sharp' \rightleftarrows D'$ $E \rightleftarrows D'$

195.

(a)

$F\natural' \rightleftarrows D'$

(b)

196. The Laird o' Drumblair

In Strathspey time

J. Scott Skinner

RECOGNITION SQUARE − 6

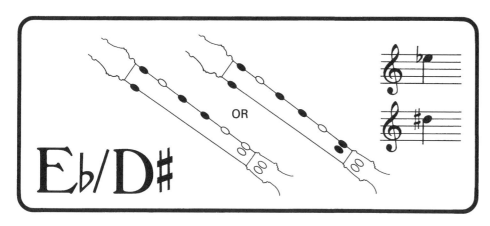

E♭/D♯

OR

— the second fingering (with R3) is better in tune on many recorders.

E♭ ⇌ D

197. Play this and the next exercise (a) tongued
(b) slurred overall

E♭ ⇌ F′

198.

199.

Play (a) tongued
(b) slurred as shown

200.

201. In the fields in frosts and snows

low F ⇌ E♭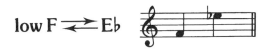

PRACTICE CIRCLE for E♭

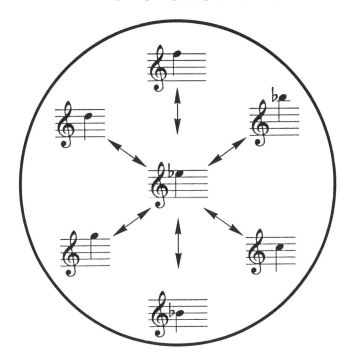

202. Sinfonia from 'Almira' (part)

Tempo di Minuetto   Handel

mp legato

203.

204. The Scale of B♭ major

(a)    (b)

205. The Lorelei

With a gentle swing

German

206. The Scale of G melodic minor

207. The Scale of G harmonic minor

208. Down among the dead men

Con spirito

English

209. French Carol

210.

211. The Arpeggio of C minor

(a)

(b)

212.

*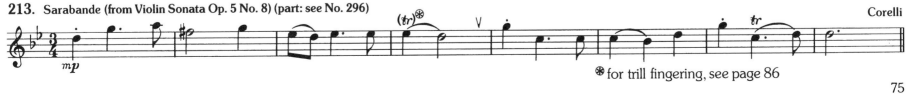

can be a useful fingering for G′ between E♭
and B♭′ in fast passages.

213. Sarabande (from Violin Sonata Op. 5 No. 8) (part: see No. 296)

Corelli

✸ for trill fingering, see page 86

214. When we were young

Allegretto

□ German

215. Giga from Sonata No. 7 in E♭ major (part)

Presto

□ Schickhardt

216. Courante from Sonata in B♭ major (part)

Lively

□ Handel

tr etc.

B♭ ⇌ E♭

217.

Allegro (eventually!) (V) for slow practice only

□

218. Gavotte

D♯ – though fingered in the same way as E♭, always seems a much easier note as the more troublesome shifts to and from E♭ do not occur with D♯ in the keys you will most often meet in recorder music. The following exercises give practice in the simpler moves. C♯ – D♯, perhaps the most awkward shift, is reserved for a later chapter. (See Part 2, page 100)

219.

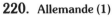

220. Allemande (1)

221. Allemande (2)

Susato

222.

223.

224.

225. Weep not I pray (part)

Welsh

B' ⇌ D♯

226. Russian Tune

Allegro

227. Going with Deio to Towyn (part)

Briskly

□ Welsh

B ⇌ D♯

228. The Arpeggio of B major

(a)　× 3　□

(b)　× 3　□

229. The Dominant 7th of E major

× 3　□

230. The Miller of Dee (part)

Allegretto

□ English

231. David of the White Rock (part)

232.

233. Go no more a-rushing (part)

234. The Marsh of Rhuddlan

235. Old King Cole

Con brio

English

— the 'middle five' fingering.

Ab′ ⇌ G′

236.

Ab′ ⇌ Bb′

237.

238.

Are you still playing exercises of this type with varied tonguings?

239. The Scale of C melodic minor

240. [Ab′ ⇌ B♮′] The Scale of C harmonic minor

G′ – Ab′ – Bb′

241. 3-part round: Hi, ho, nobody home
Moderato

☐ English

82

242. There in the meadow

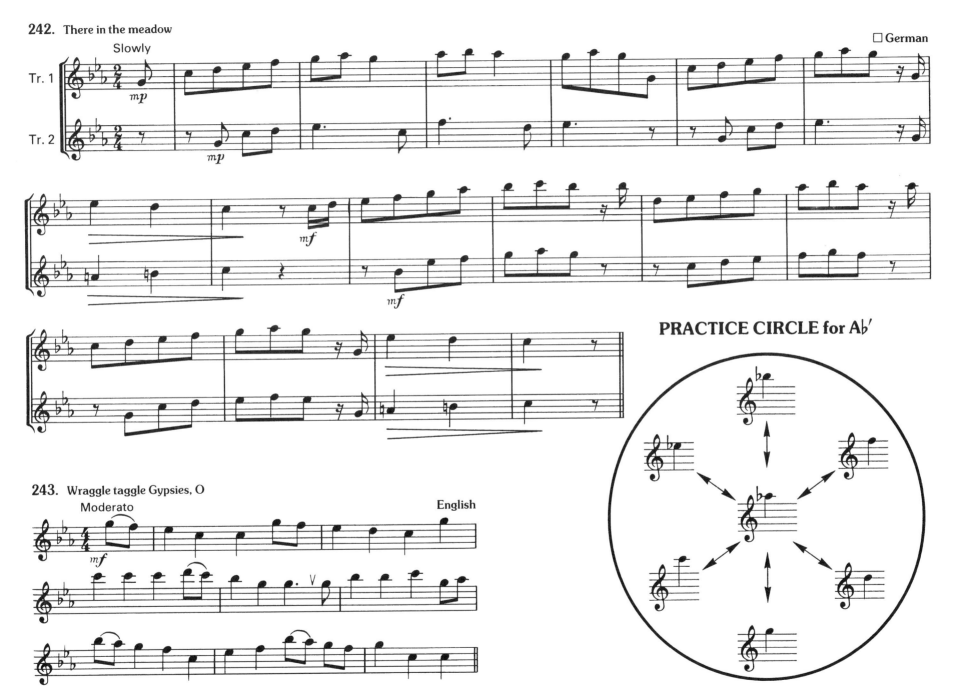

243. Wraggle taggle Gypsies, O

PRACTICE CIRCLE for A♭′

F' ⇄ Ab'

244.

$\times 3$

245.

$\times 3$

246. Coventry Carol

Larghetto

English

_p_ legato

247. I went through the greenwood

Brightly

German

_mf_

84

248. Minuet

Poco allegro

Corbett

*originally

⊛ E♭ – D trill

E♭ ⇌ A♭′

249.

250. Up the Raw

Allegro vivace

☐ Northumbrian

251. Divertimento in E♭, K252, 4th mvt. (part)

Mozart

Presto assai

G#′

A′ ⇄ G#′

252.

253.

×3

254. The Scale of A melodic minor

255. [F′ ⇄ G#′] The Scale of A harmonic minor

* F′ – E♭ trill

● (if used)
○ for E♭

 A′ – G#′ – F#′

256. Ca' Hawkie (part)

Allegro con brio

☐ Northumbrian

257. To the Maypole (part) (cf. Part 2, No. 237)

Con spirito

☐ English

PRACTICE CIRCLE for G#′

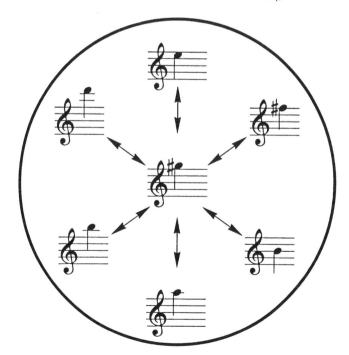

E  G#′

258. Nos Galan (part)

Brightly

☐ Welsh

B′  G#′

259.

260.

261. Liebster Jesu (part)

☐ J. R. Ahle

Slowly

262. Menuett

Fischer

D → G#′

263. Larghetto from Sonata in A minor, Op. 1 No. 4 (part)

Handel

* originally notated in $\frac{3}{4}$.

⊛ see opposite page

There is nothing more frustrating than finding an attractive piece of music well within your capabilities − *but for a couple of unknown notes!* The four-movement Sonata for 2 Trebles (Op. 1 No. 12) by Mattheson, from which the following Rigaudon comes, is a case in point for, with your present technique, you could play it all were it not for one or two brief passages involving upper E and lower C#.

It makes sense, therefore, to press on and learn the remaining notes of the treble's normal compass without delay, for they will open up so much more music to you. You will find them in Part 2 of this book, together with more splendid tunes and some particularly enjoyable solos, and I hope we may meet again then.

B ⟶ G#′

264. Rigaudon (part)

Mattheson

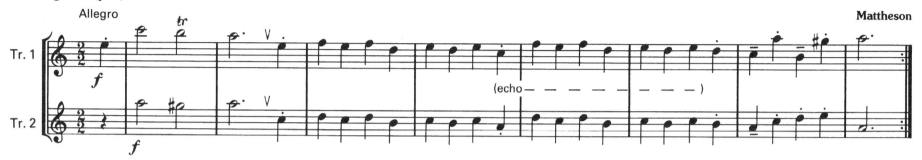

* A′ – G#′ trill

(For a useful list of the most frequently
used trills, see Part 2, Appendix 3)

INDEX OF TUNES (Part 1)

2 Two-part settings

* Christmas carols and songs

o Rounds

Acknowledgements

The author and publisher are grateful to the following who have allowed copyright material to be used in this book:

Oxford University Press	Christmas Pastoral by Robin Milford
Messrs Kalmus Ltd/ Theodore Presser Co.	With care I tend my rosebush